THE POEMS
OF AUGIE PRIME

THE POEMS

OF AUGIE PRIME

GEORGE WALLACE

WRITERS INK PRESS
New York
1999

For book orders, contact: WRITERS INK PRESS, Post Office Box 2344, Selden, Long Island, New York 11784. Phone/fax 516-451-0478.

Acknowledgements
I would like to express my appreciation to William Heyen, Maxwell Wheat and Phil Asaph for their help in editing this manuscript. I would also like to thank *Confrontation*, *Back Street Editions*, *Killdeer*, and *Nassau Review*, in which some of these poems previously appeared; and the CW Post Library Association, for awarding first prize to *An Old Fishing Village at Dawn* in its annual Community Competition.

International Standard Book Number
0-925062-19-7
A **3WS** *Edition*
First Edition
abcd

Designed and produced by David B. Axelrod, Publisher.
Printed by Peconic Company, Mattituck, New York

Contents

BACK TO SCHOOL

Pinioned, as he was, by a backpack full of books
not twelve steps past the garden gate
and fifteen from his mother, the young child
stopped to admire the color of dahlias
in the late-summer sun,

an action which was not to be considered
a matter of elation, but more specifically
of one who had become deliberately lost
in the overwhelming pulchritude of nature
as it disgorges its human young
into the schoolbuses of autumn —

all this was not lost on his mother, as it happens,
who had to sweep him up the huge steps
and into the stewardship
of a cigar-smoking driver named Mel
who had driven this route for more years
than anyone here could remember
and would certainly not

consider the idea of standing around
idling his engine
for any child he considered to be

dawdling.

THE OLD MEN

have taken back their harbor just this morning
now that the youngsters have returned to school.
Half-bent over the white fence rail
and their hands hold fishing line.

Perhaps they expect some miracle of fish
to emerge from out of the oily gray: but
it is more likely that the gingerbread reflection
of the biological lab buildings across the harbor

will leap up from the dull surface
in a nineteenth century spray of history
than to expect that anyone will catch a fish today.
No matter. Just a few weeks previously —

though it was at night — three teenagers
mingled in the same damp spot
which, being spelled out in a salty script
of their own devising, must remain

indecipherable to the casual passerby.
Or to the old men fishing pierside
in September. The tree is known by
its fruit. They cannot explain why.

SOME SEPTEMBERS

It feels like summer
will go on forever.

This one for example
well into the middle of the month
and you can tell it's going to be a hot one.

It is not exactly the stillness of the morning air

I guess it is the way
all across the neighborhood
locusts are buzzing like defective
electrical appliances, and one crow

starts barking over by Ezra's pond
the way they did centuries ago, when Matinecock
told time by the crows. Oh, and off
in the distance, it is in the way

a lone motorboat scuds across the harbor.

Somehow you know the summer heat
is going to be oppressive on mornings like these
even though it is mid-September.

There! In the eave beyond your line of vision
a dove moans. You moan once, too —
if the air would only just move!

This is about the time that,
chucking the window up one last notch
trying to draw a broader breath

you finally discover exactly how it is
those hornets have been getting into the house.

ON THIS PARTICULAR MORNING

the man of the woodlands wakes up
and it is autumn, and he is amazed
at how fast his feet and leggings become soaked
in the tall grass

when not so long ago it was all a wild clinging on
of seed and insects in the dry summer sun

But now it is morning and he wakes up
and the leaves and branches
he chopped from the walnut in August
smell like cider along the trail. The man

of the woodlands breathes it in, and deeply,
expecting the usual intoxication. Instead
his breath returns, in a clean and quiet
exhalation of clouds,

into the general decay of the forest.
There is more dignity in the heavy going
of the red maple, with its wet, rusty leaves
that nearly touch the ground, now ready

for another brush with death, he reflects,
there is more dignity in that, than
in the raucous combat of God knows
how many crows on Kettleback Hill,

in the linden trees — so the man of the woodlands
decides he will not take a swing at the red maple

on this particular morning. No! on this
autumn morning he will head for Kettleback Hill.

AN OLD FISHING VILLAGE AT DAWN

There is a time of day
in the earth's remembered stillness
when the sun breaks hazy over the left shoulder
of the oversized remains of an industrial building
and geese hold steady to their pre-flight positions,

forming up in memory of previous migrations
out across the flat gray harbor.
A time of day when fish by the dozens,
you can hardly believe it, come flipping
out of the meager, almost expressionless,

face of what many in these parts
consider to be dead water. Guess again!
Between the semi-yachts and the last true
fishing boats, before the swirl of oil
and suburban commotion can spoil

the morning, a whole school of fishes,
predators themselves at the moment,
and some of them quite full-bodied
for harbor dwellers, break water
and in such numbers that a seagull,

which had been floating peacefully
somewhere mid-harbor, is suddenly
compelled to take shelter on a pylon
close to shore. It is at times like these
that I walk home with the Sunday paper

and warm rolls tucked under one arm,
encouraged by the continued presence
of two pigeons pecking their way
down Main Street, and this unexpected
communication of life from the harbor.

And am content, by God, to ignore
the sun's weak performance in the October sky.

SHELL PICKING IN AUTUMN

I like to see what the shore has gathered
on a fall morning, before the first frost.
A sudden march of blue mussel shells, the tattered
victims of an underwater storm, or in the lather

a bright yellow balloon some child evidently lost
and must have bothered mommy for, halfway home.
They say that autumn is the cost of having
lived so marvelously in summer — as for me,

forced by the inevitable rotation of the fickle sun
to roam in cool shell-picking time, I'm not
complaining. There are those of us who own
a temperament more suited to the splashing

struggle in the foam, the daring lunge
into the hot sea, the strong body straining
against the waves — or even how to tempt
that "kiss me" pout from pretty girls

as they go strolling past. It is my fate,
or misfortune, to be one more suited to this
short season's claim — the wistful recollection,
as the sun heads South. The great settling out.

EXPERTISE

A notch should be enough
to fell all but the greatest oak
in the prescribed direction

yet when the powersaw's chain chokes
into the underbellied softness
of a treetrunk, gives the merest suggestion
of resistance, or else succumbs to the pinch,

it is all I can do to keep my footing,
give in to jackrabbit fear, and quit
cutting. It is apparently no good

to remind myself that a short distance
away, between the trees, my neighbor is sitting
behind his safe, and perfectly composed,
picture window, watching. Or that the chainsaw

owner's manual has specific
reassurances for every situation
imaginable. I read and re-read

nearly every inch of the thing,
but as such things go, this is my first
episode with an instrument of such
obvious fury, designed to destroy

second chances. Use
lessens marvel, this I know.
But when it comes to saving a little
wear and tear on the merchandise, not to mention

thumbs, a little expertise would also be nice.

INDIAN SUMMER

Knocks on our roof like angry walnuts.
Speaks in the rustling of these leaves,

taught to spear the white moon, bloodless
against the window's cheek. Listen:

bluebottles sinking in the creek.
If summer has disappeared, there are none

in this house as know it. Listen.
Ten thousand locusts, if one, singing

in a field of dead corn. What hope
tonight for the good sleep of October,

the effortless floating off, or the sweet,
chill rising at dawn, ready as ever —

like the men of the orchard — to pack apples?

FALL'S NOT ALL IT'S CRACKED UP TO BE

How soon the brave leaves of autumn give over,
transformed into a gay sort of wind-litter

the trees are having their last fling
in the cheerful slanting sun

but when November stops with the nonsense
and plays its hand, it is a mad sort of letting go

this leaping from the maple branches.
And you would leap with them, wouldn't you,

with this glad army of leaves parachuting
into the sun. It mesmerizes you, doesn't it,

until you see the cold aftermath,
the horrifying result. Will you look at these —

trace after trace the white crystals frosted
to the veins, why all this leaf-skin is no longer

green! You can barely tell where is that
good autumn color? In the gray slatternly

morning without sun, a most unattractive one,
at that, and frozen to the ground, breath

of the crystallized air gathering at your nostrils,
the strange suspicion that maybe

we have done something terribly wrong,
after all.

BITTERSWEET

So much tension beneath the surface,
the earth's churned terrain, that November
weeps with it. The skin of the thicket

breaks out into a rash of orange blotches.

In the heat of summer, reduced to
hog sweat in the weft and wattle of its rooted
origins. Engaged in a two-fisted tug-of-war

full knuckled in the dirt, I have. The futile puzzle
is this: to do battle on its territory, or succumb
to the seductive lure of its devices,

the trill and brattle of a brisk winter breeze,
chattering among its yellow-capped tendons.
Fools decorate the hearth with snippets,

garland the shelves and chill windowpanes
with its twigs and tempting berries. Better
by far to steer clear of it altogether.

Or, offered, a sprig, to simply toss it.
Given the chance, it will choke everything
in its path. Before God and the world

we have named it bittersweet.

STREETSWEEPERS

The sky breaks gray, to drizzling rain
which must have been lurking just outside
my window, long before November. Autumn again,

and the maples are pasted with rust. Even Tom,
my alleycat, is afraid to let go of his sanctuary
below the roofline of the porch, and venture out

to his cat-work. I cannot blame him really. Out
in the street, the rough idling of great yellow
machinery is to him a warning more real

than the petulant chattering words of a nervous
sparrow. Mornings such as these, the wise
know enough to stay in bed, and dream. Yet

men in streetsweepers, fortified with coffee,
in rainslickers and an extra pair of dry socks,
forget the weather report, start their engines,

and commence cleaning. *There's more
than that to life, eh lad?* I tell old Tom.

And letting fall the curtains by my bed,
I watch the rain take exercise of the season.

CAR TROUBLE

Isn't it enough that the overcast sky pelts
the pavement, flays the chestnut trees with wind

and rain tonight? Idling rough like this,
in front of *Henley The Metal Fabricator*'s shop,

the damn engine has to up and quit
and I find myself walking, fast as the approach

of midnight, curb to corner, not even slowing
to decipher the sharp accent of barbed wire,

or graffiti. In this neighborhood, there is no cause
for anything you would actually call words.

Whether or not it is smart for a man like me
to walk mean streets like these, this

is evidently my moment for it. I recall the old advice,
with respect to the reversal of fortune, which always

worked best, according to the old man:
stick to low mileage vehicles, principally.

Steer toward the main roads. Keep well clear
of strangers walking alone at night. Above all,

avoid reflection. It is now that I recall the wisdom of
the old man's words, and decide it is best to heed them.

FIRST DAY OF WINTER

For weeks, I heard the winds erupt
in a furious autumn concert of trees.
Fields of them, knocking heads in a fit

of natural selection. First, the snapped twig,
then came branches breaking,

and finally a self-destructive tumult
as if maddened from pursuit, over the hilltop
hurtling the overwhelming invasion,

the wind's illimitable army, whole
stands of them, in harm's way, tree trunks

giving over. Now it is time for the other voice.
Winter. Still as a dog's whistle on Jayne's Hill.
Icy, invisible, but as ready to do its job

as lies, icicles, or else, perhaps, the surgeon's knife.

SUCCESSION

I do not mind so much the blank look
on the face of dawn over the brittle fields,

the grass covered with white stipple. But when
first frost comes to the late-blossoming daisies,

I recognize what it means to be summarily tossed
aside by the season, as something irrelevent —

a thing designed for an undemanding season,
like spring, possibly even summer. This is winter:

the days of frozen birch have come. All
that was gentle is lost beneath a fine frost.

Now the wise old squirrel hides himself
in the cracked ribs of trees, or underground.

We will not see him again before the thaw,
when he comes out to consider the latest realities —

like who gets to nest in the maple,
and where are those acorns hidden?

SNOWED IN

Pale light
and the bedroom curtains —
at last we are content indoors.

Nesting
on new fat pillows
stuffed with gosling feathers

we lie
in warm wait
for the snow's fine hissing

against the roof
and aluminum siding
to start.

This book I shall read
if it takes all night.
With any luck

we'll be snowed in by morning.

SLEEPWALKING: ICE

Winter is something that happens while
you're sleepwalking, and the black sea
which is the sky is round and full of moon
and suddenly the stars which you never
even noticed are all a-pop and rattling
with the cold, with each shuffling step

you take, and it starts you wondering
What is that clatter? Could it be
the flat end of a truck bouncing
off of outcropped rock, could it be
the manhole cover, could it be
it is none of those? I remember

how the sunlight seemed to blind my eyes
it just froze me for an instant — that
was the dream where we were skating
out by the salt box house and the sucking wind
ached in my teeth, it ached all down
my throat, and I looked back to see

who that was who was calling me and the ice
began to bubble began to boil and I was falling

in every direction at once and the water
ached all down my throat and I wasn't
blacking out just yet but I was about to black out
so I kept staring hopefully at the hole

which was hanging up there in the white sky
and that's when your hand reached in those fat
welcome fingers and you pulled me out
and there I was shivering and awake.

As if I never even knew you existed! As if winter
had slipped in under the treeline, unexpected!

DROWNING ICE

My brother discovered
brand new ice, a cap
of ice, it was, out back,
forming in a plastic bucket.
Round as a silver dollar,
and near as thin.

He pushed it in
with the end of a shovel
just to hear the ruckus,
wet and hollow,
of drowning ice.
What a sound

in the winter sun
as he tipped it in
again and again
with a terrible grin,
the little devil.

Not at all
a nice young fellow,
little brother.

SENTINEL

How is it that the crows know
to strike such a dignified pose
atop the winter trees, now
that they are bare and the earth
lies wasted and frozen

along the bald hills which border
this parkway? Yet here, when you
least expect to notice them, sit the crows,
square against the snow-heavy sky,
muffled by its great gray coat.

You would think the way we stare
it would startle them into flight. No!
This is the moment when it is the fate
of certain birds to stand tall in the aviary saddle,
and compel the passing motorist to tap his brakes.

Or failing that, at least to let up on the pedal
for a closer look. In this case, we settle
for a single crow on the top branch, because
it breaks the monotony of leafless trees.
Perhaps they are no more than a kind of stubble

on the face of the hills, the crows — yet even
that will do in January. A few black feathers
catch our eyes, it seems, if only because they
are the one thing that does not conform
to the general pattern of winter, and the big freeze:

Unremitting. Uniform. Hard as concrete.

DEGREES

This sloping field down to the harbor
has seen neglect far more
dramatic. Yet, impressed like this
against the winter sky, one empty nest

in the upper reaches of a tree
commands my attention. How could it be
there are so few nests to go around?
There must be twenty crows or more to be found

patrolling the grass, not to mention
a nameless flock of black dots down at the harbor.
Reason dictates there be, for every
so many birds, a nest. My one among twenty

suggests there is a poor soul somewhere
who must endure the sight of twenty
nests and only one bird, by day. Or worse,
in the winter night, when all depart to a single

roosting stand of wood, where thousands flock,
sullen crows in deep congregation. It makes
for certain, cold comfort, in the drift
of winter days outside my kitchen window

not to be so alone by day, or so invested
by night. Makes, in fact, for just the right
degree of crow companionship, taking it
as I have chosen to, as a way to count myself

among the fortunate.

OVERCAST

First thing this morning
branch tips shake

chill wind
penetrates the walls

a bad sign

no trace of shadows
yet I know

something
is definitely stirring

in forest corridors

a neighborhood dog
sniffs

the air gives chase
up the hill

his short legs churning

dumb barking beast
knows something

I can't imagine
casts a shadow

where no shadow falls

SNOWCAP MELTING

Ill-fitting white wig
no holly tree could ever bear.

And all slipped to one side
under its own weight,

now that the sun has come out.
Thought you were a wedding veil

on the head of a pretty bride,
did you? Well, we all know

thinking doesn't make it so.
Fate could have made you

king of the snowdrifts, mounted
you high as rooftops, and as wise.

Not you, sag bag. Oh not you, Prince
of snow muffins. Not you, snow drip!

IMPRINTS

The smell of wood smoke at dusk,
the feel, through laced boots,
of blue snow crust
breaking with my every step. Above all
the coming of night, and you.

And the earth's letting fall,
through a century-old wooded path
down to a seawall by this harbor,
the moonlight. Now add to that
the salt smell of winter.

There is nothing cruel in weather like this

despite our shared reflection
on the effect of ice, which creates
plated mounds where beach grass grew
with profusion in summer. There is nothing
cruel in the complacency of snowy hillsides,
deflecting heat from the sun all day,
though it may contribute to the cold.
For us, this winter night, what is true

and valuable is how we humans collect,
beneath a watchful moon, each to each;
how you gather yourself to my side.
Or how we walk together

in watchful silence along a frozen harbor.
Here, for example, where I take the imprint
of your body on mine. Here, where we measure
the pulse of a star's persistent warning. Here.

IT IS NOT ONLY IN THE BOTANICAL GARDEN

of Brooklyn
that ice in new plates
stacks itself

end over jointed end
like a deck of oriental playing cards

on the carp-bottomed pool
of this Japanese garden
ice forms tonight

by the light
of a blue lantern

she leads you to the parking lot

the moon rises in a rice paper sky
it is shining through a wedding veil

there will be snow tonight
she smiles

you reach for her hand

TWO SMALL BOATS

in winter twilight
and the parent
in me asks

where is the child
to do the rowing
under this sickle moon

where is the child
to mount the tide
to tipple on ice

where the son, the daughter
to cut like cable
through water

cut through ice
through a season
like this

where there is no parent
you may yet find
the child

CALLIGRAPHY

Quilting at your lease and leisure
by a curtained window in March.
A clock ticks in now and again, asking
only that its presence in the entire fabric
of the season be decidedly known, by any who visit
the quiet of this well-cushioned establishment.

In January, we were too flushed with the remains
of Christmas cheer, and debt, to notice.
By February, all memory of how we got into
this mess — another coarse, hostile winter —
had been obliterated. We didn't even panic
when the house turned strange, and began pulling

dark, looming faces down the terrible corridor. No
matter. Now it is March, when the worst that winter
offers is drenching rain, or a sudden expanse
of snow when you don't expect it. Soon the sun
may even shine with conviction.
By now, we have become accustomed to the limits

of weather, and to the certain comfort lamplighting
at dusk can bring. In April, reconciliations will,
no doubt, have to be made. Like who left the cat out
and why we no longer chase daisies. But this
is March. Here, by lamplight, we apparently agree,
for you have taken to your quilting. As for me,

I confess it. I am considering, for the fifth year
running, the benefits to be gained in learning
the patient art of chinese calligraphy.

I'LL TAKE MY WINTERS COLD

I like to see the old men gathering dry sticks
in early March for firewood, along the highway;
the stubborn spray of small branches, miraculously
strapped to their backs, the pull and catch of wind

and sunlight streaking throught their hair. There
are lessons for me in the gay air of defiance
which I detect, watching their jaunty movements
through woodlands thick with cherry stumps,

with ancient maples. And that's another thing. I like
the trees — how they show in winter the way
they have bounced back against the action of vines.
It is written in a kind of bold script, the supple,

patient survival machinations, which helped trees
get through summers of clinging vegetation.
I understand that in this world there are those
otherwise reasonable people who would choose,

given their preferences, Februaries that are filled
with sun and leafy growth. For sure, that sort
of action's well-suited to summer and youth. But
winter's when we learn to appreciate the survival

of the old against the odds. I'll take my winters cold.

FORSYTHIA

When did spring ever come
when it was supposed to? Set to start,
some interference of the gods
brings on an icy rain so numbing
the forsythia go into tailspin.

Other years, it's a matter of sun
coming on with such strength it incubates
the wet and broken remains
some seagull, or perhaps two terns,
left at tidepool's edge. There are those who learn

as it goes, to dress for the occasion,
follow the hesitant dance step
of March winds. They've got it measured
right, I suppose. For me, weather
is still a matter more of taking chances

than measurements. Like forsythia, which shoots
blossoms when its sap says "go,"
regardless of the seasonal passage of light
and moisture. Forsythia — which, guessing right,
erupts like ten thousand suns, in bright profusion.

Or guessing wrong, comprehends the truth
of the matter, and plays possum.

IN OUR GARDEN

There shall be flowers
where there are no
flowers now

ask the crocus, which
knows it: ask
the snowdrop

the white moon
which slices through
March and the night sky

is letting fall fantastic
petals without
number

you and I
shall catch them
soon, very soon

GREENING OF THE WILLOW

Winter, do your worst!
It is spring
and the greening of the willow
cannot be thwarted.

The trees and underbrush
in the hills above this northern harbor
are sporting new outerwear,
all those tight fists are gone green.

Whose head is that I see
peeking through that forest floor?
Jack-in-the-pulpit
has parted the brown leaves

or else a hyacinth,
heavy with musk, which has sprung
through a charley chaplin hole in nature's
old woolen pants!

Another March has slipped past
like lost luggage down a long
lonely airport corridor,
nothing but an old man's curse,

more threatening than true.
Goodbye, old tyrant winter!
This path runs to summer,
and away from you.

CROPDUSTER

When I first heard the single engine airplane
rum-drumming outside my bedroom window

like a movie victim's Studebaker rolling
headfirst down the slopes — slow-motion

of course, hurtling down some California canyon
in black and white — I was afraid. That soon

changed. *Only a cropduster!* I laughed. It is
mankind's huge return to sky, and the memory

of agriculture, fields, and the great maneuvering in
to deliver some payload. A mist of fertilizer,

perhaps, or more likely seed this time of year.
A cropduster, skimming tops of trees, in true flight,

and taking me under an imaginary sun,
where I shall spread dream seeds, and once again

become — yes! — a man of action in spring.

STOPPING AT COLD SPRING POND

roll down the window
peepers she said

thousands of them
chirping at pondside

you can smell the water
shallow water

even in the dark

just then the tuneful night
burst into stars

*i didn't hear them by the
harbor* she said

we must have been facing
the wrong direction

into the face
of this old whaling village

into the past i ventured
instead of spring

SERIOUS SPRING

When flowers first give over to leaves
the serious, interior work of trees,

the adding on of girth to pulpy rings,
begins. This is also the season when,

on their knees, gardeners normally begin
to dig their way down sunny furrows — asking

nothing else of earth but fertility
within the boundary of their individual fences.

How alone and proud they stand in each garden,
rolling up white-buttoned blouses by both sleeves!

Meanwhile in town, Main Street toughs also heed
(surreptitiously, at least) the promise of spring —

I know this is true, don't ask me how — and quietly
each notes with pleasure the budding of trees.

I suppose each of us somehow must believe
that our own miraculous response to spring

is beyond the comprehension of skeptics. But see
how so many and various thrive in nature's moment

as if in a dream beyond the swaggering beauty
of first blossom. This is a thing of mystery! This

is serious spring.

SPEAKING OF SQUIRRELS

Ring around the moon means rain. Fishermen
have nets to mend in spring. White oak tells us

when to plant corn. Speaking of squirrels, how
about those two gray acrobats inventing

personal roadmaps twenty feet up? I guess
high above the bobbing heads of daffodils

is where squirrels were meant to be — scattering
on wide-beamed elms, barking about.

If I could take their cue in April's sun, loud
and blue, and cast off into impossible nets of wind

as squirrels do — above the celebration of flowers
never to fall with a thud into the forest? Well,

squirrel freedom would be mine too. But
as it stands, this particular brand of life's pleasures

is denied me. God apparently is content
in his heaven. He's keen on having some of us

plow their little plots of earth between trees
while others — rats in fur coats actually —

flaunt gravity and the rules of wingless flight.
Some say it is only a mad futile gesture at the

great mass of sky. Perhaps. But for eloquence,

the sudden flight of squirrels in the forest
is some of the best I have ever seen.

GARDEN SHED

Old black shingled rooftop!
you supported me, a perch above trees
when I was twelve. With a rebel yell
from your sparkling eaves, I leaped
into supple branches made soft with leaves.
While others took chances on the popular fields
of sport and combat, you were a nest
to me, and taught me the ways of treetops,
as high and alone as a bird of prey.

Now, swallows nest in rotted
bits of you. The trunk of an old walnut
has rubbed graffiti into your one good eye.
As for me, I could scale your side
with a single leap, should the need arise.
Yet when the afternoon sun flays itself
into little crystals on your back like this,
I see you as I did at twelve —
and I wonder, can I still do that bird whistle?

Heck yes. I haven't forgotten.

NORTH SHORE

A land made tall by its trees.

Hidden in rooftops
the crow recalls a cruel punishment
which the sea endured on rock-heavy shores
to the west.

Summer cries
like a teakettle in the neighbor's kitchen.

Hoping to capture the sound of crows,
I step outside into wet morning grass —
and discover, instead, the pawprints
of a neighborhood cat.

This bird sang until it was bidden.

A DOGWOOD SAPLING MADE CLEAR

of the twisted battle for sunlight
on the edge of the thicket
will right itself in as little as one season.
Not at first, mind you —
but before your average gardener
has time to start cursing,
the green tips of new leaf will pop out,
promising riches in a direction

formerly occupied by honeysuckle vines,
silverlace, and the like. Imagine for yourself
a new window opened to the sun! Wouldn't you

tend towards it? In a few months, tendency
has grown into intention; your young,
tenderleafed stems are climbing skyward
against a grain which now exists
only in sapling memory.

As it happens, I know all this to be true —
because on this land, I have been the one
to set a dogwood sapling free. Skinny, perhaps,
but no longer overcome. And by this, I have learned
that nature, in the form of a dogwood tree, at least,

in adversity may seek only survival —
but given its freedom, it will strive for something
higher: balance. Which is to say that Philosophy,
it now appears to me, sometimes requires

the intercession of an outside hand. Especially
in modest grounds such as these,
so badly in need of clearing.

WEST HILLS

Soil so rich you could plunge your hand
up to the wrist in it
like so much sea foam
tossed up from the stormy harbor.

With just one thumb
he could dig a furrow through it.

He gives a nod
toward the hills beyond,
and another
at the sun, banking down into the seas.

All good farmland, and a home
for carpenters, says he,
to the tune of the jug and fiddle.
Just like the artist showed it.

So Van Velsor says: *If the jug spills*
ignore it —
drink or no, this upland soil
don't snore.

Take heed of that, son.

GRADUATION

Young girls and honeysuckle
cluster at the edge of schoolgrounds
and at rusted chainlink fences
like these, swapping strong perfume
and dangling long-grown legs
thinly over life's edge in June.
The young art of blossoming! We all
succumb to its tutelage in summer.
The first blush of color rising
to the lips; the body, confused
with strange heat in new places; and
the overwhelming urge to simply chuck
all the annoying stuff of textbooks!
Come summer, what once served as guideposts
has become fences. Come summer,
to grow becomes to go beyond fences,
even into the unsafe woods, to seek
the source of honeysuckle — to graduate
into the great disorder of things,
to taste the unrefined sweetness
of wild places. Surpassed, perhaps,
by the subtlety of garden roses,
but as yet untamed by the tired hand
of human cultivation.

SUMMER CULTIVATION

The first step defines all others.

Which is why I visit garden centers in Spring.
I like to speculate
on the red and white possibilities
that sticks of rose bushes, or azalea
rooted in bags of soil, may bring
to the dark spot I like to call my garden. Of late
the rage is all impatiens, I observe. Like
the scrubby weeds that already inhabit
my garden, they tend to please when blossoming.

This fine flower, I reflect, began as a weed.
As have all, I suppose. And left in my garden
to fend for itself, would soon return to the wild
or die, no doubt. Still, I cannot be too concerned
with death, when summer returns. This is
shovel time, when cultivation attends my days,

early and late. This, I say, is no time
for pondering fate. Let the digging begin!

LOCUSTS: A SUMMER TRYPTICH

1.

Proud as the descendants
of the Northern Europeans
who first settled this town
to build ships. And as remote.

By most accounts, a direct hit of lightning
will not kill them.

What is Ginko, or a Japanese Maple,
after all, compared to the likes of these?
All the way down Woodbine Avenue, you can
see them rise up above the rabble
more recently arrived.

2.

To judge by their rough trunks
you would think them prehistoric.
Certainly, the texture of their bark
suggests worries quite ancient in origin.

Then too, consider the leaves! Impossibly
out of fashion, one might say. Quite
frond-like, while today's preferred ornamentation
is decidedly deciduous.

3.

In the hurricane of '38, I'm told,
dozens of them came down, ripped out of the earth
by their shallow roots. Yet today, they continue
to march without apparent interruption
or consideration of the past, Christian
as ever, and erect, straight down Main Street
to their precious harbor.

MULBERRY TREE

So puny a trunk I wouldn't have noticed
if I had accidently cut it down that season
when everyone said I went mad in the bushes,
levelling everything not clearly marked *tree*

with my new and very expensive garden tools.
What a fool I'd have turned out to be! In the rush
toward sunlight, in pursuit of that suburban
lout, market value — which cultivation

supposedly brings — to have axed this sad sack
of the forest. These are motives at odds
with the mulberry's more modest truth — berries
from a tree. Though gardening books cast doubt

on the durability of its fleshy fruit, I take my cues
from the birds out back, and their mad singing.
Testimony like that has always served me well, if only
to supplement the logic of gardening encyclopedias.

NIGHT FISHING

dusk following rain
in a field with three horses.

night has finally settled in
on one black knee.

steam rises —
soon it will be fireflies.

between the necks
of horses bent to water

venus, descending,
listens for the sound of young boys' laughter.

whenever stars
drop in to see their own reflection

we catch them.

MIMOSA

Things bidden fail to thrive, generally,
in the thicket. Here it is all a very natural
sort of germination. By June's end,
there has already been a procession of the usual
vines, a few wild roses, and knotweed.

Then from across the garden border
come hundreds of mimosa seedlings,
straight out of the garden apron, and they make
an absolute mockery of my delphiniums.
Still and all, the earth must be supervised.

And I don't mean bulbs — the squirrels
apparently feel it is their duty to uncover them.
Nor is it poppies — they need too much sun.
Decidedly, I was chosen to inhabit this spot
on earth to tend mimosa. My yard is absolutely mad

with them. As to where the seedlings come from,
I've never been apprised. For all I know,
mimosa seedlings follow me. What I do know
is this: despite having joined the struggle,
I am surrounded by frond-covered ground

year after year. Fact is, it is a fate I have learned
to endure. In maturity, mimosa break out into
a most unusually delicate flower —
plumage a South American cockatoo, no doubt,
would be proud to wear in some sweet-smelling

jungle. A gardener of mimosa, me? Things
could be worse. The task, at least, is in accord
with the forest order. Who am I to question that?

HORNETS' NEST

I discovered it
by accident
sitting under sassafras
between two sweetgum trees.

The neighborhood cat
and me
stung to find
perilously placed

so close to home
a hive —

more a giant's head
cheeks like yellow
lantern paper
than a house for hornets —
five thousand years of

Chinese civilization
could not manufacture one
more economically
without an abundance of
inexpensive flowers.

Just listen to that satisfied buzzing!
Must be some flowers
to please bees
like that I tell the cat.
Which ones?
But the cat's gone.

I'm thinking catalpa.

CATBIRD

At first, it was a promising morning — but now,
the temperature has risen too many degrees.

In the hedge, catbirds mimic summer thunder:
a signal, perhaps, of a break in the weather?

When July comes, it is enough to occupy oneself
indoors, counting the beats of a ceiling fan.

See how this one sends the squares of sunlight
on your bedsheet so sweetly shuddering.

Yet the one who is proved most wise in summer
is the one who seeks shade, not shelter —

like this catbird, singing in our hedge. Let us
go there, now, and seek the fortune in his tune.

ORDER IS HEAVEN'S FIRST LAW

But this is the forest, Father James. Where
variation takes precedence. An unexpected possum
up a sweetgum tree, for example,
which sets even the most knowledgable
dog barking. Are you aware, for example,
that there are those among your student monks
who regularly, down by the harbor,
disrobe in summer
and dive naked from the pier?
Despite the water's familiarity
with the monk's nude progress,
each dive disrupts the muddy surface
of the salt marsh, as they disappear
into the hooded, mysterious darkness.

On earth, things are ever changing.
Consider lightning, intolerant
with things being left
the way they have always been. Clergy
and Destroyer to the forest, some call it.
Or consider a baby's patient attempts to smile
at the strange thing so lately identified
as Mother's face. Each proceeds
according to its own rhythm of discovery.
A new mystery is revealed among earth's
ten thousand things, or in the variations
found within each one of them. And we rush
to solve the conundrum.

Did you ever wonder if the dictates of heaven
aren't seriously reversed on earth? We celebrate
the more curious acts of monks and babies,
possums in trees, cherishing the great and various
unpredictability of a mixed hardwood forest
sloping down to the shore. Confusing? To be sure.
But in the hereafter, Father James, there's
time enough to fathom the startling organization
of earth's brave things. Take my advice —
dive now; we'll sort things out after.

WAKING BEFORE MIDNIGHT

Now summer, there can be
no doubt about you.

Lying in deep sweat I count how you grow.

Numb with crickets
surrounding strange rooftops with singing.

Summer your stars twitch westward
in the rippling night.

Your jackal has come
to devour the savannah moon.

Why has the neighborhood gone swimming
under a green halo of maples?

Summer, the wicked hum of air conditioners.

I will race your street tonight,
shooting out streetlamps.

US CRICKETS

hunt by day
sing by night
hang out in the tall grass

life can't be all bad
lawnmowers pass right over
almost everything worth mentioning

consider this:
fourteen hornets two moles
one green walnut lying in even greener grass
and us crickets

someone made lawnmowers to pass over all these

if it wasn't a cricket god,
it should have been. someone
keeps sending lawnmowers our way
to remind us that life goes on all around

no matter what men may do
to keep up appearances
and their tidy little schemes

lawnmowers are the cricket god's punchline
they leave us laughing

COMMERCE

Three geese head east into dawn.

It has been summer so long
my sister's swing hangs limp in the morning.

Now cicadas sing the end of night from every tree.
And crows recommence, from a tall beech,
their pointless squabbling.

As for the sun, this morning
it is tending to the treetops.
Full of itself, not even summer can stop

its own success. Yet once perfect, things fade.

Hoe corn while you may,
sang the Long Island whaler,
in teeming waters, and distant to our harbors.

One might do well to pray for his deliverance
from the broad harvest of hurricanes.

FIRST LESSONS

What with the lanes of every hill and hollow
littered with leaves, and most gutters
choked with twigs and grit,
you would think every late-summer storm
was a force-four hurricane.

But trees and windstorms never seem to mix.

These days, fire and rescue personnel are out
seeking fame and bragging rights. As for
electric company linemen,
what they have to say
a few hours into a major storm
does not, I'm afraid, bear repeating.
Volunteers may love hurricanes.
But for linemen, it's earned pay.

Meanwhile all afternoon, my neighbor has been
sitting windowside, quietly reading. If,
from time to time, she checks
the status of an apple tree,
or a stray trash can, she will deny
worrying that anything could be uprooted.

Perfect excuse for a good book, she smiles, with
North Shore composure. *No electricity.*

As for the neighborhood's sons and daughters,
your average August squall spells
the end of summer. These are the days when,
with the end of freedom looming,
nature and the school year first teach our children
the meaning of loss.

These lessons linger. To me, this smell of wet leaves
glued to asphalt, as the world surveys its brave
wreckage, is as much recalled as it is new.

BOTTOM OF THE HEAP

that's where
the action is

this stuff
turns to soil you know

if it doesn't rot
expect the bottom of the pile
to spread its wings
expect it to fly

might be soon
might be not

but one day
turn a hot spadeful
see what you've got
see what's taking root

meanwhile
whatever is on top
has nowhere to go
it just sits there baking
in the august sun

imagine that

this compost pile
makes me smile

fermentation
triumphant

RIGGING OUT

Years go by and the men of the village,
sons of fishermen mostly,
have apparently forgotten what the harbor
even smells like.
And then one evening,
Leo rising gingerly in the east,
the idea of rigging bursts into their horizon
like a star.

By daybreak, you find them standing harborside,
two by two, dozens of them,
practicing their sea knots, in rubber boots.
All this time
the harbor has been talking to itself
against the sounding shore. Now, someone
is listening to it again
from the sand. This one wanting, perhaps,
to avoid putting oar to water without
certain assurances.
That one, perhaps, simply joining in.
Dinghy. Wharf. Luff. Swell.

When the game is afoot, it is good to cast
for names like these, if only to recall
the way Old William's reliable
mud channel works itself through
the marshes, or where to find
that drop-anchor spot
which was always the best place
for catching flounder. As for the going,
I am sure the sea
will always be a thing that must be learned
each man to himself. But when it comes to words,
it is another matter.

Ask the men of the village, spelling out the tide
in the alphabets of their long-lost fathers.

BIRD WADING

not an ibis — but there is something in the muscular bend
of his prayerful neck
that recalls in crooked letters the still banks of egypt

he works the leaping channel
for his supper

a low tide so full with mud, sun & mussel shells
the world is become
all blue shimmering luminosity

it is a wonder he can keep himself
so white

across the harbor a churchbell rings
our lady queen of martyrs
calling someone to prayer or celebration

three bells & two old men
seated by the railing

their necks bent in rare devotion to bait buckets
fishhooks & brown bottles of beer
they are just waiting for the tide to roll in

soon it will be them
fishing

BLACK EYED SUSANS

I see the bright face of this our still young and hopeful nation
more in a parking lot weed than in the display
of its proud public gardens, untamed as the original
North American wild, outwitting us to the last
& filled with the breath, a continent wide,
of unplanned vitality.

In the lowest dandelion, in the fairy clover,
in the dusty sway of goldenrod where two highways merge,
the ragged memory of prairie grasslands calls out to me
& praises still sung to the sun rippled expanse
of northern forest.

I leave to Europe the curve and grace
of horticultural refinement, manicured intention
& tired topiary imagination & rather, stoop to worship here,
even at this crumbling bit of curb,
your voice, America — stubborn, plain, strangely

triumphant. So long as a single unplanned flower
raises up its head to greet the expectant sun,
I too shall greet, in celebration, the promise
of your ragged, wonderful world, which is the reason
why we came here in the first place

& yes! pretty as a patch of Black Eyed Susans.

About George Wallace

A native Long Islander, from an early age George Wallace was raised in an oak wood hillside overlooking the Long Island Sound. Over a period of twenty years he worked and studied across the United States and abroad before returning to Long Island in 1988.

It was during his early youth that Wallace gained a lifelong appreciation for the magnificent bounty of Long Island's North Shore coast. Throughout his youth, Wallace spent many hours and days, in all seasons, absorbed in the atmosphere of the coastline and wooded uplands his family called home. It is this experience which has informed the persona he adopted in his Augie Prime poems, written as a calendar sequence and based on his observations of the progress of the seasons through a single year's cycle.

Wallace's previous volumes of published poetry include *Tie Back The Roses*, Explicitly Graphic (UK), 1986; *The Milking Jug*, Cross Cultural Communications, 1988; *Tales of a Yuppie Dropout*, Writers Ink, 1992; and *Butterflies & Other Tattoos*, Bootleg Press, 1993.

For over a decade George Wallace has been a lead writer for Walt Whitman's *The-Long Islander* and is a four-time New York Press Association Writer of the Year nominee. In addition to hundreds of critical articles on the arts on Long Island written annually, he regularly reports on the range of stories effecting his community.